CRACKERS

THE INCREDIBLE TRUE STORY OF A LITTLE DOG WITH A BIG JOB

HILARY DRYSDALE

Foreword

I decided to write this book after one of the many visits back to my homeland of Zimbabwe, where I met some local people who weren't familiar with the story of "Operation Noah": the incredible wildlife rescue that took place on Lake Kariba in the late 1950s and early 1960s. They were especially enthralled by Crackers – the little dog that became such an integral part of the rescue effort – and were amazed that they had not heard his story before. I therefore decided it was time for this brave, unassuming, crazy little dog to be documented and immortalised: hence this book, and a statue of Crackers to be found standing proudly on Fothergill Island at Lake Kariba.

Operation Noah was one of those events you can hardly believe took place. In the late 1950s, the then-Rhodesian government dammed the mighty Zambezi River to create a hydroelectric power station. The government had forcibly relocated the Batonka people who lived in the area as construction of the dam wall began. But as the new lake formed, it swallowed up thousands of square kilometres of bushland that thousands of animals had also long called home. The animals' fate was almost an afterthought, until the Rhodesian Game Department hatched the plan that became known around the world as "Operation Noah". Over a period of about five years, a small team of men rescued and relocated more than 6,000 wild animals that had become stranded on the islands that had formed in the lake. These helpless creatures would otherwise have drowned or starved to death. The operation lasted from 1958 to 1964.

Because my father, Rupert Fothergill, was head game ranger of the operation, I am lucky enough to have access to many newspaper articles, photographs, diary entries and 16mm film footage he recorded of the action, as well as personal accounts from descendants of some of the men who were there. Unfortunately, with the passing of time, fading memories, and the imperfect nature of record keeping, I will have inevitably failed to include everyone who played a part in this endeavour. For this, I apologise. If you, or any family members, were involved with Operation Noah, in any capacity, please do join our Facebook group dedicated to the memory of the project: facebook.com/groups/operationnoah

As for this book – where details of Crackers' life are unknown, and occasionally to help with the narrative structure, I have taken some artistic licence for the sake of the story. However, all key events described really did happen, and at the end of Crackers' story you will find historical pages providing further context and photographs supporting those stories, and of Operation Noah in general.

Video of Operation Noah can be found on YouTube.

Hilary Drysdale, 2025

Sculpture by artist Joyce Correira erected on Fothergill Island, Lake Kariba.

Contents

Forward		ii
Prologue		vi
Chapter	1. Pup in the Pub	1
	2. The Adventure Begins	3
	3. A Multiskilled Mutt	5
	4. A Humbling Encounter With a Honey Badger	8
	5. The Porcupine	11
	6. A Hyena, a Dead Leopard, and a Hero	12
	7. The Black Mamba	14
	8. Rescuing a Rhinoceros	16
	9. The Lioness	18
	10. Winding Down	20
Epilogue		22
The Story of Operation Noah		24
Acknowledgments & References		55

Prologue

The great Zambezi River had flowed through the valley for thousands upon thousands of years.

For much of this time, the surrounding land had been home to the Batonka people. They were subsistence farmers and hunter-gatherers, by all accounts a loving and peaceful people, who believed in Nyami Nyami – the River God.

But times had changed and their homeland now had a government, and the powers-that-be had decided to build a dam and hydroelectric power station at the town of Kariba. This would provide power for the country's growing population – but it meant forcibly relocating the Batonka people from their traditional lands before their homes were flooded.

Africa's animals lived here too, and as the waters rose, they were becoming stranded on the small islands that were forming on what would become the planet's biggest man-made lake. There was no plan for their future – until there was: upon realising the catastrophe that would befall these innocent creatures if they were left to fend for themselves, the head of the Rhodesian Game Department, Archi Fraser, pulled together a band of men and assigned them to "Operation Noah": the most ambitious wildlife rescue operation since the biblical flood of Genesis.

The men had one heck of a job to do. They were to head out in armadas of small boats, come up with creative methods to capture the stranded animals, transport them across the water and release them back on the mainland. Their terrified and desperate cargo included lizards, snakes, leopard, lion, porcupines, warthogs, antelope, zebras, monkeys, rhinos, honey badgers and just about everything in between.

Humans had caused the animals' problem, and humans would be their saviours – humans, and one plucky, lucky, little dog.

The Kariba Dam wall shortly after completion in 1959

The Ark heads 'Operation Noah' flotilla

Dedicated to all the men and women who worked or volunteered on Operation Noah, and those often overlooked wildlife saviours of today who still work so tirelessly for the betterment of Africa's wildlife.

Chapter 1: Pup in the pub

The little dog knew he should be happy with his lot in life.

He had a home, a kind owner, was well-fed and looked after, yet yearned for something more. Chasing butterflies around the garden wasn't quite enough. Real adventure was his dream.

The pup knew he was small in stature but felt he was destined for big things in life. Little did he know that big things would soon be coming his way...

The owner of the dog, a man named Bob, had been working on the new dam that was being built near the town. Sadly his contract was up and he was moving on, but couldn't take his pup with him.

So one night, before Bob was due to leave, he took the dog to the noisy pub on top of the hill where the locals and workers liked to congregate for a meal and drinks. Bob sat at the bar with the dog sitting at his feet, looking up at him quizzically. The little dog's rather dull and boring life was about to change drastically.

Bob downed a few cold beers and banged on the countertop with his fist to silence the crowd. Once he had their attention, he picked up the little brown mongrel and put him on the bar counter. The patrons stared at this curious specimen, with a long body like a dachshund, short little legs, and a fiery fox terrier attitude.

In a loud voice, Bob told the crowd that he needed someone to take the dog or he would have to shoot it. The little dog didn't think he could be serious, but gave a plaintive cry just in case.

As it happened, there was a group of game rangers in town, they were from the Operation Noah team. Everyone had heard about the important and exciting work they were doing, rescuing the stranded animals from islands in the newly forming lake and releasing them onto safer dry land.

The men had come back to the mainland for supplies and were gathered at the bar for a drink. One of the rangers, a man named Tinkey Haslam was there with his wife Margaret. They had only recently lost their beloved Rhodesian Ridgeback, and sensed something special in this little dog.

Tinkey downed his ale, stuck his hand up and shouted "I'll take the Heinz 57!". The whole bar cheered. It was the mutt's lucky day.

From the moment the little dog left that bar at Tinkey's heels, his life became one big adventure.

Chapter 2: The Adventure Begins

The little dog sat in the back of the truck as the game rangers drove away from Kariba. He watched the town disappear into the distance as they headed for the Operation Noah base camp at Peter's Point, set up in a small clearing in the bush on the edge of the lake not far from the new dam wall.

Upon arrival at the camp, he bounded out of the vehicle and raced around, exploring and sniffing in every nook and cranny of the site. The men had slept in canvas tents at first, but now some had round huts with thatched roofs. They laughed as the little dog, yapping in delight, ran circles around them.

The excited pup introduced himself to each member of the team by pressing his wet nose at their knees but it was Rupert Fothergill, the head game ranger, to whom he firmly attached himself.

"Come on little fella, time for some rest. We have a big day ahead of us tomorrow," Rupert told him. They would be heading out at first light on a rescue mission.

The little dog curled up at the foot of Rupert's camp stretcher, closed his eyes, and dreamed of all the adventures that awaited him.

By sunrise, the camp was all action. The maps were out, the boats were loaded with boxes of fresh supplies, cooking pots, fuel, tools, tents, mosquito nets, weapons, ammunition, and medical first aid kits – everything they the team would need for their time on the islands. A lot went into the capturing of wild animals that didn't understand they were being 'rescued' from the slowly rising waters, and generally didn't take kindly to the ordeal.

The boat engines started up, and all jumped aboard including the lucky dog. The excited pup quickly claimed a position balanced on the bow of the boat, where he had the best view of the horizon ahead.

The rangers laughed at his audacity.

"This dog is completely crackers!" Tinkey said. "In fact, he needs a name – and Crackers seems just right."

With unanimous agreement from the others, Crackers became the little dog's official name, and as the flotilla headed out across the waters, so began his role as the mascot of Operation Noah.

Chapter 3: A Multiskilled Mutt

The first island the team stopped at was full of impala and some of the smaller ground animals. The men first set up camp, then toiled in the hot sun rigging long stretches of raised nets all across one end of the island.

Crackers sat back and watched in awe as the capture took place – the men quietly spread out in a long line at the other end of the island. Then all of a sudden, the cacophony began: the rangers marched along beating pots and pans like drums, shouting and hollering and hitting the scrub with long sticks, making as much noise as possible to flush the animals out of the bush. Scores of panicked antelope and warthogs, zebra and bush pigs were caught up in the drama. They unwittingly ran towards the trap and became tangled in the rope webbing.

The men did their best to soothe the terrified animals, as they gently pulled them out of the nets and secured their legs with nylon stockings. They ear tagged each one and loaded them onto the next boat leaving for the mainland.

This was certainly a lot more exciting than what Crackers was used to seeing! But he didn't just want to spectate – he wanted to get involved. Fortunately, he soon found a way to make himself useful…

The one place the men couldn't get to – that Crackers easily could – was down antbear holes. These underground havens were often gatecrashed by other animals seeking sanctuary, and until Crackers was on the scene, the men had been at a loss as to how to extract them.

The little dog knew what had to be done: he would sniff at any antbear hole he came across, and if he detected any animals hiding within it, he would bark to alert the rescuers. Then, without any regard for his life, he would zip down the hole and chase them out.

The men would stand at the ready, waiting for Crackers to hastily back out in a cloud of dust, followed inevitably by some kind of angry creature – often an antbear, pangolin, or honey badger. Sometimes, several animals would emerge from the same hole. On one occasion, Crackers was chased out by a warthog, tiny gemsbok, baboon and antbear.

The waiting game rangers were stunned by his natural ability and intuition. Crackers was soon seen as a key member of the team – as important as any of the men.

Crackers gained a huge sense of satisfaction out of having a job to do, and soon discovered he had another talent – but this time, his work was in the water.

He had observed that some of the larger antelope – such as sable, kudu, and impala – were not always as grateful to their rescuers as one would expect them to be. They weren't aggressive animals, but in a panicked state they became a little unpredictable, and their horns could cause serious damage. So for safety's sake, the rescue team would release them in the water close to the shore, rather than on dry land.

The problem was, the animals were sometimes so panicked they became disorientated. On one of these occasions, a small herd of antelope were released in the shallows, but started to swim in the wrong direction, heading right back out into the rising waters from which they'd just been rescued.

Crackers leapt into action: He jumped overboard and swam around the animals, yapping and rounding them up like a sheepdog would in a paddock. Much to the rangers' relief, he guided them to the safe dry ground that would be their new home.

Chapter 4: A Humbling Encounter With a Honey Badger

As the months went on, Crackers' confidence grew and he was involved in the rescue of a large variety of animals. He would often be the last on an island sniffing around to make sure the team had not left anyone behind.

One hot summer afternoon, he had almost finished his final sweep of an island the men had been working on, when at the bottom of a small mound he found a young steenbok ram with sharp little horns staring back at him. The little steenbok had a baby face with a black spot under each eye, which made him look sad. It was frozen still in terror – Crackers tried to communicate that he was there to help, but the steenbok's instincts told him he needed to urgently remove himself from this strange yapping animal with four short legs and sausage shaped body. He'd never seen anything like it in the African bush!

The steenbok zigzagged its way down to the water's edge with Crackers in close pursuit. It plunged into the lake and swam as fast as it could, with Crackers following closely behind. The men had already started loading the boats for the mainland, so Crackers herded the steenbok up to the edge of one, until it was close enough for the men to reach down and lift it safely out of the water.

The men reached down for Crackers, too – but he was already swimming back to the shore. He had a feeling there was more to do, and returned to the mound where he'd found the steenbok.

Sure enough, there was an antbear hole on the other side of it, and Crackers could sense there was something inside. Eventually he flushed out a stubborn warthog which he chased to the water's edge where the rescue team were able to contain it.

Next out of the hole came a demonic honey badger. This furious creature taught Crackers a tough lesson about getting too cocky. When Crackers rushed right up to its face, barking obnoxiously, the honey badger latched onto the little dog's nose with its razor-sharp teeth and refused to let go. Crackers' pained yelping drew the rangers quickly over to help. Rupert gripped the honey badger's jaw and squeezed tightly to release it – slicing his palm open deep enough in the process that it would leave him with a lifelong scar. The honey badger's teeth were prised out of Crackers' nose, and the men put it into a cage to prevent it from doing any more damage. Crackers made the most of this opportunity, taunting the snarling honey badger from outside the bars of its prison, until suddenly his attention was taken by the next creature to emerge: an equally perturbed porcupine.

Crackers ran from that porcupine as quickly as his short legs would carry him. With his nose still swollen and throbbing from the honey badger's fury, he didn't fancy having any sharp spiny quills piercing his rear end. He raced to the water's edge and leapt into one of the boats, leaving the men to deal with their prickly charge – and hoping he never encountered one again.

Chapter 5: The Porcupine

Crackers was out of luck. It was on the very next island, and at the end of a long day, that another porcupine presented itself. The weary men found it hidden in some shrubbery, and were relieved that this would be the last animal to return to the mainland before sunset.

They awkwardly grappled with it, eventually securing it in the sack and loading it onto the last boat. It was then they realised their canine companion was conspicuous by his absence.

Crackers had taken off at the first whiff of the porcupine. He was still nursing his injuries from the honey badger and had no interest in acquiring any additional puncture wounds. He'd fled into the bush and found a shady spot where he stopped to catch his breath. But fatigue and adrenaline got the better of him, and before he knew it, he'd fallen asleep, dreaming of the supper that awaited him back at the main camp.

The men called and called for the little dog, but got no response, and the light was fading fast. Eventually, they had to leave without him. It was a strange and sombre journey back to camp without their mascot sitting on the bow of the boat.

Crackers woke up at dusk and raced down to the shore, but the men and the boats were nowhere to be seen. He was overcome with shame when he realised he was all on his own because he'd run away from a challenge. As the night sky filled with stars, and the air filled with the sounds of nocturnal life, he chided himself for letting fear get the better of him. This life of action and adventure was all he'd ever craved. He swore if he ever found his team again, he'd make up for this lapse.

Chapter 6: A Hyena, a Dead Leopard, and a Hero

At first light, Rupert took a boat back to the island to search for Crackers while the rest of the team prepared for that day's rescues.

He walked through the bush calling out for the dog, and finally came to a clearing where he was confronted with an astonishing sight: he could see Crackers' head sticking out of an opening between two rocks. A metre or so away, a snarling hyena was staring the little dog down. Crackers stood his ground, growling back at the hyena. It was one heck of a showdown.

Then Rupert noticed what the hyena was really after – a dead female leopard lay mangled on the ground just behind Crackers. The hyena scampered away when it saw Rupert, and Crackers came flying out of the gap, tail wagging furiously. Rupert gently chastised the mongrel, while also patting him with relief at finding him alive – a little city dog would have made an easy meal for any number of predators in the night.

The ranger walked over to the dead leopard, curious at this unusual sight. Leopards, being apex predators, do not normally fall victim to other animals. But the spoor and other signs left on the ground told a story: Rupert saw the big footprints of an adult elephant, and the smaller prints of its calf. Close by, were some marks where it appeared the baby elephant had been knocked over. It seemed the leopard had taken too big a risk for its dinner, and fell victim to a protective mother. A sad sight, but a reminder that the natural world was full of brutal drama.

Rupert started to head back to the boat only to realise that Crackers wasn't following. He called the little dog's name sharply, but still Crackers held back, seemingly trying to tell the ranger there was unfinished business here.

He walked back to where Crackers was standing, and followed the little dog to the crevice in the rocks where he'd first had the standoff with the hyena. Inside were three tiny leopard cubs with half-opened eyes. They were spitting and snarling, but too tiny to hurt anyone. With their mother now gone, they had no hope for survival without help. Rupert picked them up and carried them in his hat – they would have to be hand-raised with the menagerie of orphaned animals back at the main camp.

On the boat back, Rupert marvelled at the little dog's instincts and bravery. There was no doubt that Crackers had put his life on the line for these three cubs, and had more than redeemed himself for his brief moment of cowardice the previous day.

Chapter 7: The Black Mamba

Crackers enjoyed a hero's welcome back at the main camp after the incident with the hyena and the leopard. But there was no time to relish in the glory – the waters were rising with every passing day, and the rescuers were quickly back into the swing of things. Besides, there was no shortage of drama and excitement to fuel further war stories for the team. At times, it seemed as though they were on a life-or-death merry-go-round, with either Crackers saving the animals, the rangers saving Crackers, or Crackers saving the rangers.

As some islands began disappearing altogether under the rising waters of the lake, many animals were becoming stranded in the treetops. The rescuers would slowly manoeuvre their boats up to the spindly branches poking out of the water, and pluck out of them desperate chameleons, legavaans, monkeys, genet cats, nagapies (bush babies), and even birds and their nests full of eggs.

On one occasion, they were pulling up to get close to an exhausted monkey hanging from the last dry branches of a mopane tree. All eyes were on the weak little creature, when what appeared to be a thin black twig suddenly sprang to life.

Crackers instantly clocked the threat, as the deadly black mamba moved as quick as a strike of lightning just above Rupert's head. The little dog sprang from his position at the bow of the boat, and snapped his teeth across the snake mid-air. Both fell tumbling into the water, and after what seemed like a very long time, Crackers surfaced with the snake in his jaws.

The little dog was the toast of the campfire again that night, and thought back to his days chasing butterflies in the garden in town. In hindsight, that had been quite good training for his new life!

Chapter 8: Rescuing A Rhinoceros

Crackers had been involved with the rescue of just about every type of animal so far, so was most put out when one morning, the rangers considered leaving him behind for that day's rescue. The thing was, they had a rhino to deal with that day. And of all the wild and dangerous animals the rescuers dealt with, perhaps none was more intimidating – and seemingly impossible to capture – than the rhinoceros. Rhinos are notoriously aggressive when cornered, and besides all that – weigh well over a tonne. Even if one could be somehow lifted into a boat, it would sink it!

The rangers had come to realise the only way to relocate rhinos was by first sedating them with a dart gun, then hauling their slumbering mass onto a custom-built raft and floating it across the water to the mainland. They couldn't see what role Crackers might play, but in the end gave in to his pleading eyes and let him come along.

They were soon glad they had: this particular rhino was determined not to let the rangers get a clear shot at its rump. They had it cornered at the edge of a small island, but the furious animal was whipping around, snorting and pawing at the ground, making very clear its intentions to charge – horn first – if the men did not leave it alone.

Crackers decided to solve the problem by playing decoy: he ran right at it, barking underneath its nose. Rhinos are very short-sighted, and when the dog came close enough to fall into focus the rhino zoned right in on the strange creature, forgetting about the rangers for the moment. Crackers' entire body was about the length of the rhino's horn – this was not an even match, and anyone putting money on the outcome would have to bet the dog would come off second best. As the rhino swung its head from side to side, it seemed any moment Crackers would be ripped to shreds, or tossed to the tree tops.

Rupert yelled "Turn him! Turn him!", and somehow the little dog understood exactly what he was to do. With his tongue flapping against the side of his mouth he eased forward even closer to the rhino, and held its attention completely, moving around slowly inch by inch so that the rhino was forced to turn with him.

Soon, it was standing side-on to the rangers, and Rupert was able to fire the sedative dart directly into its rump. Over the next several minutes, as the drug took effect, the rhino became unsteady. Crackers ran about dodging in and out of the great beast's legs, until eventually the rhino slumped to its knees, narrowly avoiding crushing the little dog under its weight. It then rolled to its side and became still, allowing the team of rescuers to safely prepare it for transport back to the mainland.

Legend has it that Crackers sat on top of the rhino on the raft, looking exceptionally pleased and proud of himself.

Chapter 9: The Lioness

Rhinos were one thing – but even Crackers had the sense to realise lions were no ordinary cats, and that he'd do best to keep his distance until the men had one contained.

He sat back quietly in wait, as the men set a trap with fresh bait inside. Once the smell became too much to resist, a lion entered the crate and the door was dropped down, so the cat could not escape. At this point, Crackers started feeling brave again – cheekily yapping at her from outside the cage.

The men threw a tarpaulin over the crate to calm the animal, and dragged it to the water's edge before loading it onto a raft. Most lions accepted their fate, and lay quietly sulking in the cage for the journey to the mainland. But this particularly angry lioness was most indignant about being in custody – and stirred up by Crackers – and roared the whole way across the lake.

When it came time to release the lioness at the mainland, the rescue team decided for safety's sake they would use the same methods as for some of the larger antelope, and let her jump off the raft and swim to the shore. Crackers surprised everyone, by jumping into the water right after her, making sure she made it to dry land.

Mission accomplished, the lioness turned and gave one last resentful roar, as Crackers returned to the boat and took his position sitting proudly at the bow. Even after all these years of rescues and close encounters, he could still leave the men shaking their heads and laughing in disbelief.

Chapter 10: Winding Down

The rescue team sat around the fire, having their evening meal in a reflective silence, with Crackers at their feet. The next morning, it would be time to pack up camp for the last time. After nearly six years of Operation Noah, of tough, important work in the African bush, of extraordinary acts of live-saving bravery and more than a few near-death experiences, the rescue team's work was done.

They'd relocated more than six thousand animals, a Herculean conservation effort made all the more remarkable by the arduous conditions the team had to overcome, including a shoestring budget. Considering the dangers the men faced daily, it was miraculous that there had been no loss of life to the team.

As sad as he was for this adventure to be coming to an end, Crackers had to admit that he was starting to feel weary, and that returning to a quieter life did hold some appeal. He tried to concentrate on the hardships that he wouldn't miss – the army ants, for one. They would come marching in lines like soldiers with their nasty pincers held out, searching for high ground. Crackers would turn his back on them and spray soil with his hind legs to break up their formation. The mosquitos were even worse than the ants – and the only way to avoid them, was to go to the water's edge and sit with just his nose sticking out for air. Late at night, he would wriggle his way under the mosquito net to sleep at the foot of one of the men's camp stretchers – if he was lucky, they'd even let him curl up on the bed itself.

Crackers stared out at the lake, at the black silhouette of treetops against a sky ablaze with the orange, reds and pinks of a sublime Kariba sunset – a vision to which the team had been treated every day of the job.

That was something he would miss.

Epilogue

At the end of Operation Noah, Crackers went home with the same kind man who had rescued him all those years earlier at the Kariba Heights pub. He was soon right at home with Tinkey and Margaret Haslam, at their house in Marongora, where he had a far more relaxed time watching the children grow up, and perhaps chasing the odd butterfly.

It was a very sad day when Margaret found Crackers twitching and frothing at the mouth. After all those close encounters and days of derring-do in the bush, it was a snake that, in the end, managed to land a bite. Margaret gave the little dog snake bite serum and sat up with him on her lap late into the night. Sadly, he didn't make it.

Crackers is buried in the bush overlooking the Zambezi Valley, with a bougainvillea planted at his grave.

His spirit lives on in the memories of all those who knew of him and his heroic efforts with the Operation Noah team.

HERO OF KARIBA DIES

NDOLA, Tuesday.

CRACKERS, the four-legged hero of the massive Kariba animal-rescue programme, is dead. Ironically, it was a snake that killed him.

Crackers' death ended an enviable companionship between dog and man — the man being Mr. Rupert Fothergill, who risked his life to complete the operation that saved more than 6,000 animals from drowning in the rising lake.

He and his helpers owed a debt to Crackers, who took a sheep-dog's part in herding game towards the rescue armada. "Operation Noah" entailed the saving of everything from rhinos to poisonous snakes from the dwindling islands in the now-flooded Kariba Gorge. Crackers, a cross-bred dachshund, died last week.

Crackers in his retirement back at home in Marongora

THE STORY OF OPERATION NOAH

Kariba is a town on the north west border of Zimbabwe. This was the closest point of civilisation for the men who worked on Operation Noah – their base camp was set up on a peninsula jutting into the lake close to the dam wall. It was named "Peter's Point" after Peter Moore, one of the Operation Noah team members.

Little is known about Crackers' life before he joined the rangers on the Operation Noah team. Only that the story of him being given away at the pub is indeed how he came to be Tinkey Haslam's pet.

The Kariba Heights Hotel in 1958 – it was a popular watering hole for the men while they were in town for supplies.

Crackers — Operation Noah's hero

HE is golden brown with a black nose, little twitching ears and an outlandish tail that stands up and bends about the middle towards his head. He is a mongrel with a big share of dachshund. He is as cheeky as something his size dare be, brave as Jock of the Bushveld, comical as Donald Duck, inquisitive as Keyhole Kate, can swim like a retriever and his name is Crackers.

For years he was as much a part of Operation Noah as game ranger Rupert Fothergill, and during the operation that saved 6,000 animals from death on Lake Kariba he must have lived a dog's paradise on earth.

Virtually no one in Salisbury has heard of him. Certainly few have seen him. But yesterday he delighted a lunchtime cinema audience with a sparkling performance in the most recent film on Kariba's mammoth operation.

Mr. Fothergill showed it at the weekly gathering of the Rhodesia National Affairs Association. Right from the start Crackers dominated it.

Down a hole smelling out an ant bear, barking teasingly at an enraged warthog, swimming after a waterbuck or impala and then jumping cheekily on their backs, or sitting proudly in the bow of a homeward-bound craft packed with caged animals, Crackers held the screen.

DEBUT IN BAR

Even the drama of a powerful rhinoceros toppling drunkenly from a drug dart could not outshine Crackers and his capers.

Crackers's film career—and shortly, maybe, his literary career, for he may be the subject of an illustrated autobiography — began inauspiciously in a public bar in Kariba four years ago.

INTO A NET

A Kariba worker walked into the bar and asked if anyone wanted his dog, Crackers.

Game ranger "Tinky" Haslam was impressed and said he would have Crackers. And that was how his life of high adventure on Operation Noah began.

Honey badgers, according to Mr. Fothergill, are not only difficult to handle but, "I don't think they know what fear is," he says.

But Crackers was a match for them. He'd dart down a deep hole, snap and kick up a row and out they would come into a trap net.

Then he'd be seen snapping at the feet of a buffalo, his absurdly long tail cocked high in the air.

Today Crackers has only memories of the daily trips over the rising waters of Kariba Lake, trips packed with incident, excitement and adventure. But he has not completely retired. He is still in the hands of Mr. Haslam and very much a force in the Department of National Parks and Wild Life Management — although he's probably not on their pay roll.

Tinkey Haslam's wife Margaret recounted that Crackers was her "constant companion" at the base camp. She often had her baby daughter, Raye, with her, and feared that a snake would crawl into the child's pram. "But Crackers was a good nursemaid and lay next to her cot or pram when Raye was sleeping," she recalled. "He was so comical when Raye first arrived on the scene as he couldn't make out what the unusual noise was when she cried. He would jump up and peer into the pram or cot with his head cocked on one side trying to decide what this strange animal was."

While Crackers spent a lot of time with Rupert Fothergill while they were on duty, he remained the Haslem's pet, and went back home with them for holiday breaks.

Above right: Rupert with Crackers at his feet

Left and lower right:
Main camp at Peter's Point

The living conditions in the island camps the men stayed at – sometimes for weeks on end – were rustic, to say the least. Tents and mosquito nets were the basics. A canvas stretcher was a luxury, while a mattress was unheard of.

The bush and a shovel was the toilet, the lake and a cake of soap the bathroom. A hot cup of sweetened tea boiled on an open wood fire with powdered milk was a treat.

Food rations were often so meagre that the main meal of the day was regularly something the team called "sadza and point". This was the name Rupert had given to the dish, consisting of sadza, a white gruel made from finely ground maize pips, and the empty spot beside it that you pointed to, imagining meat or gravy as was the norm.

Despite these hungry times, there was always a morsel of something to share with Crackers. It was seen as a great honour if the dog accepted a treat from you.

Above: A line of rescuers making their way across the island, flushing animals out of the bush to herd them towards the nets. The man on the left is chasing an antelope, trying to guide it towards the water where capture was much easier.

Top Left: A bush pig is caught in one of the nets. Rupert Fothergill and three African team members hold it down, while Len Harvey ties its snout in preparation for transport to the mainland. Bush pigs were extremely dangerous animals, and could inflict serious wounds by goring members of the rescue team.

Left: Operation Noah rescuers carefully untangle an impala from a rope net, while another is held securely by the horns in the background. Impala were not aggressive animals, but could inflict damage with their horns in the struggle to evade their rescuers.

Nylons For The Game Wardens

Sunday Mail Reporter

HUNDREDS of nylon stockings have been sent to the Southern Rhodesian Department of Wild Life Conservation since an appeal was made for old nylons to help in the Kariba game rescue operation.

But hundreds are not enough. The rangers need thousands. The stockings are plaited into ropes to bind the legs of the animals as they are taken off the islands in boats.

If you have any nylons to spare, send them to the Department at P.O. Box 8365, Causeway, or leave them at headquarters, between Third and Fourth Streets in Jameson Avenue, Salisbury.

Silk stocking link with London

By A Staff Reporter

STOCKINGS of all shades and sizes are arriving at the offices of the department of Wild Life Conservation, Salisbury. Parcels of them are arriving from all parts of the Federation. And there was even one from London which simply had for the address: "Silk Stockings for Operation Noah."

There was no note in the London parcel of stockings, said a spokesman for the department. "There were three dozen pairs in the package," he said.

"In this country, typing schools and various business houses have collected discarded stockings from their women employees and sent them along," the spokesman added.

The stockings, nylon and silk, are being used in the animal rescue work on an island in Lake Kariba.

Since the rescue team sent out an SOS for nylon stockings about two weeks ago, in order to use them instead of biting rope or string, the department has received more than 3,000 pairs.

However, the spokesman said: "Although we are receiving a lot of stockings, we still need more."

● More stockings for Kariba will be brought from Britain by Mr. Norman Carr, a game ranger in Northern Rhodesia and author of "Return to the Wild," who leaves there this afternoon on his return to the Federation. He has been in London for three weeks in connection with his book, which was published last month. He is bringing back hundreds of pairs which have been sent to Rhodesia House by women all over Britain as a result of publicity in the Press, says Sapa.

GLOBAL APPEAL FOR WOMEN'S STOCKINGS

Many thousands of women from all over the world responded to an appeal for old nylon stockings that would be used to tie the animals' legs together during transportation. The rangers plaited the stockings into ropes which made them incredibly strong but much softer than than the coarse ropes, which could cut into and damage the animals' skin.

The rescue team wants nylons

By a Staff Reporter

AN animal rescue team on an island roaming with wild and dangerous game in Lake Kariba has sent an SOS to Salisbury—for nylon stockings.

The team, part of Kariba's "Operation Noah," want the nylon stockings for tying up captured animals. Rope and string cut into the flesh when the animals struggle.

According to a spokesman for the Wild Life Conservation department here, the island, about 40 miles up from the dam wall, is inhabited by hundreds of animals which are cut off from the mainland and are in danger of starving to death.

HAZARDOUS

Work is made hazardous for the rescuers as the island has at least six rhino and a number of buffalo.

Mr. R. Fothergill, senior Wild Life Conservation officer, and Mr. R. Haslan, are the only two Europeans engaged in this operation. They have a team of about 40 Africans.

The urgent request for nylon stockings was sent from the team's radio aboard their launch. They contacted Kariba base and the message was relayed to Salisbury.

The department's spokesman said yesterday that people wanting to contribute old nylon stockings should take them to the Wild Life Conservation offices in Jameson Avenue.

Above: Vet John Williamson and helper tag the antelope's ear

Above: A team member supports the rescued buck by its neck and feet where it has been tied up with the soft plaited silk stockings.

Right: African tracker Tembo cradles two frightened grysbok while transporting them to the mainland for release.

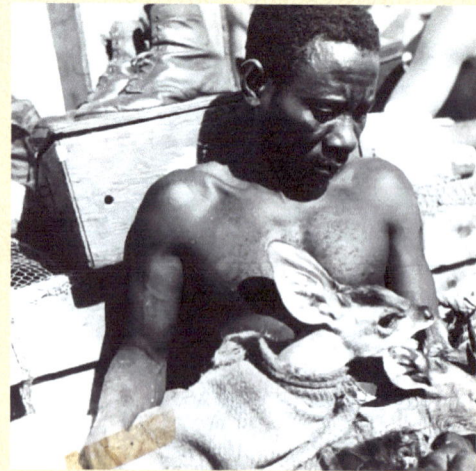

Above: Crackers contemplating a burrow
Below : An antbear hiding in the hole

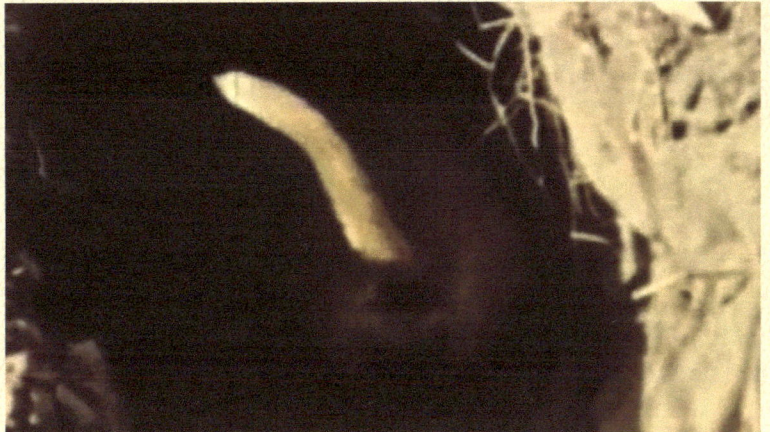

Above: Back view of Crackers going down the hole to investigate what might be hiding there. Below: Another of the residents in the hole, a pangolin

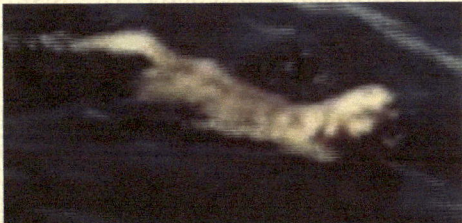

Left: Crackers in the water encouraging a herd of antelope to head in the right direction.

Right: Crackers getting a helping hand back into the boat

This is believed to be the baby steenbok Crackers chased out of an antbear hole down to the waters' edge.

An African ranger holds a rare white steenbuck.

Above: Crackers taunting the Honey Badger
Below: Porcupine exiting an antbear hole

Below: Warthog

Porcupines were one of the trickiest animals to rescue. In ideal circumstances, they were driven off the island into the water, where the rangers could catch them by their back legs with outstretched arms, avoiding their quills. They were then brought into waist-deep water, where a second person gripped the soft hair on the head of the animal, then lifted and dumped it into a sack held by a third person.

This could also happen on land if necessary, using a noose slipped over the head of the animal while running alongside it, though handling them in the water was much easier. However, the rescue team soon realised that sacks were not suitable for porcupines, as their quills often became tangled in the material and they had to be cut free. Given sacks were in short supply, and were needed for transporting other smaller animals such as pangolins, snakes and monkeys, wherever possible the rescuers used nets instead.

Strangely enough, there are no Operation records or photographs of hyenas being rescued. However this newspaper clipping reveals that at least two hyenas were rescued in 1961. A couple of theories behind this lack of information on hyenas are that either they sensed the imminent danger of the rising waters and made their way to the mainland early, or perhaps they were considered vermin and not worth precious rescue time to the detriment of the other game.

'NOAH': 2 YEARS YET

6/1/1961

Herald Africa News Service

"OPERATION Noah"—the rescue of thousands of stranded animals from the flooded Kariba area — is likely to go on for another two years.

Officers of the Southern Rhodesia Department of Wild Life Conservation will be back on the rescue work in March.

The work was halted for an "off-season" in October.

The tally of animals rescued by the game rangers stands at about 2,700—at a cost of about £10 per animal.

Almost one-half of the animals rescued during last year's operations were impala. The list included one elephant, two hyena, seven rhino, one night ape and two scaly anteaters.

Casualties were few among the rescuers and the rescued.

Rupert Fothergill holding the orphaned leopard cubs whose lives were saved thanks to the bravery of Crackers

Many orphaned animals were hand-raised at the camp menagerie, resulting in a number of cross-species friendships. Baby elephants consumed staggering amounts of powdered milk, slurping it straight from the tin with their trunks.

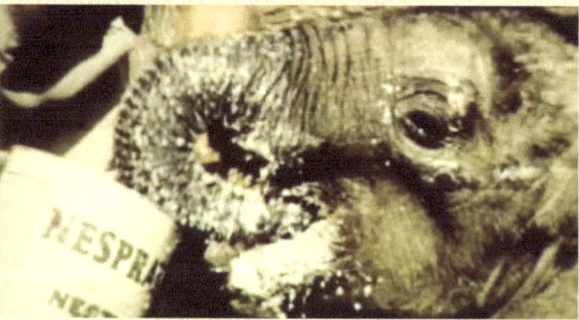

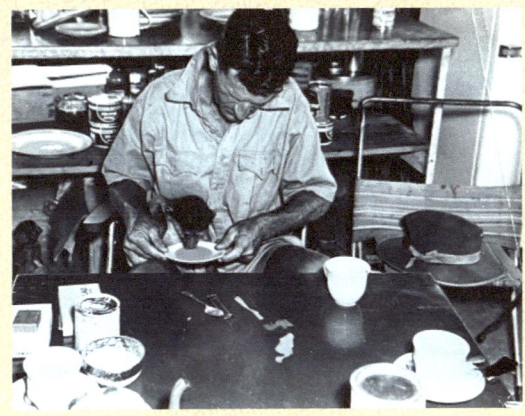 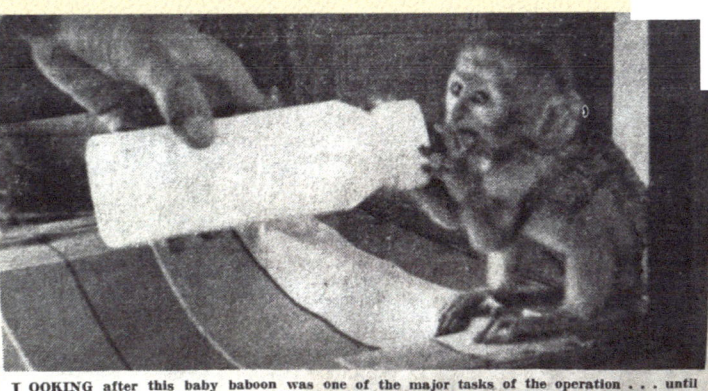 

LOOKING after this baby baboon was one of the major tasks of the operation . . . until he learned to like the bottle.

Some of the orphaned animals were sent home to Rupert's wife, Christine, to raise in their suburban home in Salisbury (now Harare). They included a hyena, monkey, baboon, young crocodile, 13 fish eagle chicks, squirrels, dassies, a genet cat, bateleur eagle, bush piglets and an aardwolf.

Likewise, one of the vets on the Op, John Condy, sent an orphaned baby rhino (that they named Rupert) home to be cared for by his wife and children.

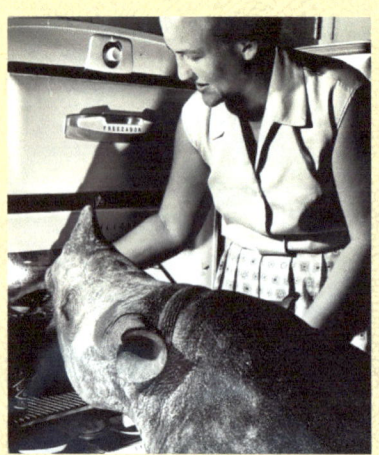  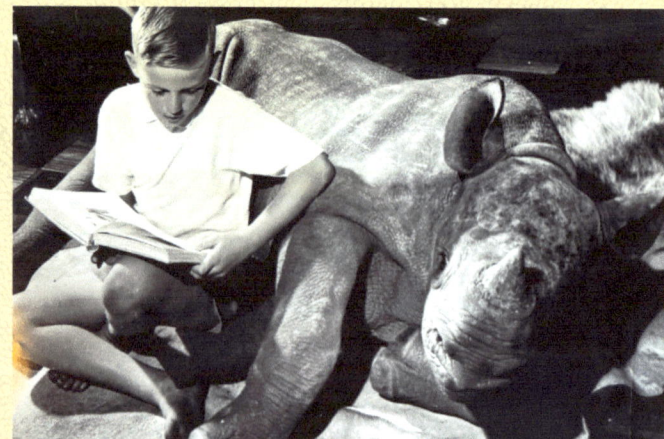

A ranger rescuing a stranded monkey from the treetops.

A bushbaby clinging on to the branches of a submerged tree.

TREETOP RESCUES

Treetop rescues were commonplace with all sorts of animals found clinging onto the branches as their place of last refuge. Ranger and scientist/ zoologist Frank Junor specialized in this area, especially with the snakes – much to the delight of the other rangers who weren't quite so keen on extracting these slithering serpents.

Left: Frank Junor rescues a black mamba.

Top Left: A genet cat clings to treetop branches Top Middle : Unidentified birds eggs in nest

Top right: Goliath Heron fledglings

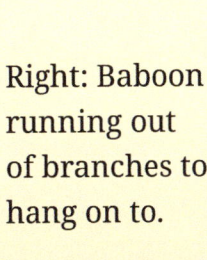

Left: a rufous-beak snake coils In a tree a few inches above the rangers

Right: Baboon running out of branches to hang on to.

Drugs had been used to a limited degree on the small game mainly for sedation and anti shock treatment. But in 1960, after many failed attempts at trying to get the rhino to swim to the mainland, veterinarian Dr John Condy and the team experimented with a dart gun and nicotine sulphate without much success.

In May of 1960 Doctors Harthoorn and Lock from Makerere University in Kampala, Uganda, came to Kariba with their expertise in capturing large mammals using drug-immobilising techniques. The drug was administered with an automatic projectile syringe or dart, fired from a distance of up to 35 yards into the muscle mass of the hindquarters. Initially the Palmer Capchur gun – powered by carbon-dioxide – was used, and later darts were fired by a cross-bow. Once the rhino had succumbed to the sedative it had to be transported as quickly as possible by raft to the mainland where an antidote would be administered and a bucket of water thrown over it to assist with its recovery.

Rupert Fothergill inspects the damage done to one of the boats by a furious rhino's horn.

Rupert Fothergill waves his hat at an ungrateful rhinoceros. The animal had been relocated to the mainland by raft, under sedation (which had to be reversed upon release), and showed its appreciation for having its life saved by threatening to charge the rangers.

THE CHALLENGES OF RESCUING LARGE GAME

Elephants sadly sometimes drowned due to their stubbornness and reluctance to swim.

Being so short wasn't always an advantage, and while there was little Crackers could do to help with some of the larger animals such as elephant and buffalo, he was always around, often pretending he was a sheep dog, and attempting to round them up and point them in the right direction.

Top Left: Trapped lioness awaits her release on the mainland

Top Right: Lioness in cage covered with a tarpaulin on its way to the mainland

Bottom left : Making travel arrangements

Bottom Right: Lioness jumps out of her cage, eager to get to the mainland. Images taken from 16mm footage filmed by Rupert Fothergill, hence the blurry quality to some.

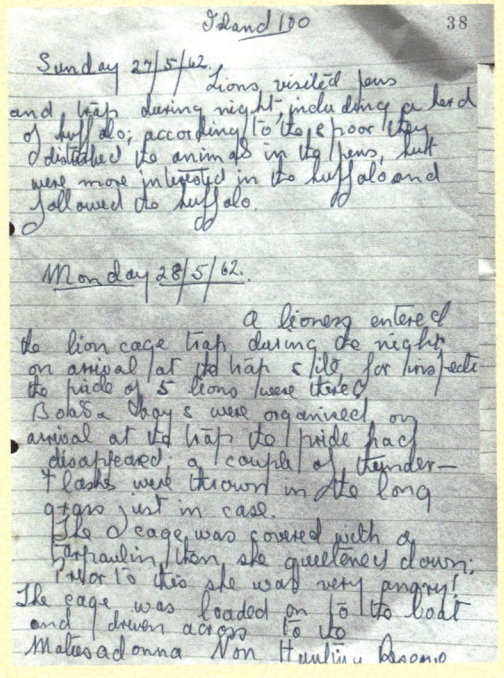
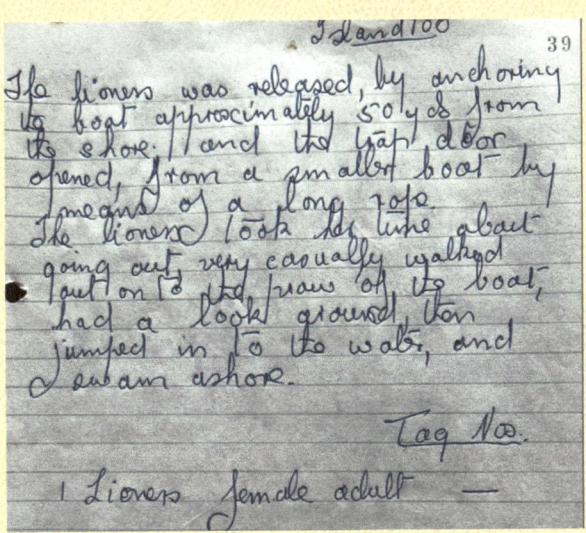

An entry from Rupert Fothergill's diaries of 25 May 1962, describing the capture and release of the lioness.

Monday 28/5/62 Island 100

A lioness entered the lion cage trap during the night; on arrival at the trap site for inspection the pride of 5 lions were there.

Boats & boys were organised on arrival at the trap ... the pride had disappeared; a couple of thunder flashes were thrown in the long grass just in case.

The cage was covered with a tarpaulin, then she quietened down.

Prior to this she was very angry!

The cage was loaded on to the boat and driven across to the Matusadonna Non Hunting Reserve.

The lioness was released by anchoring the boat approximately 50 yards from the shore. And the trap door opened, from a smaller boat by means of a long rope. The lioness took her time about going out very casually, walked out on to the prow of the boat, had a look around, then jumped into the water, and swam ashore.

Rescued..A Snarling Lioness

Sunday Mail Reporter

A snarling, viciously angry 450lb. lioness was given the freedom of the Matusiadona Game Reserve on the shores of Lake Kariba last week ... the first lion rescued in Operation Noah.

The Kariba game rescue team trapped her in a cage on an island seven miles from Kariba.

Archie Fraser, Director of Wild Life Conservation, said that the team, led by Mr. Rupert Fothergill, put the cage —6ft. 6in. high, 8ft. long and 4ft. wide—made of angle-iron and piping—against a pen which held several buck. Buck are kept in these pens until they can be transported to various game parks.

The cage was in place by nightfall, door open and cocked to close should anything go in. The rescuers hoped the open door would look like an invitation to a meal in the pen and it did.

The six lions on the island had been prowling round the pens nightly, seeking an easy kill.

The next morning Mr. Fothergill found a lioness in the cage—snarling and spitting at her captors. To quieten her they covered the cage with a tarpaulin.

The cage, built with handles well out of reach of flailing claws, had to be carried to a boat by 20 Africans—none of them happy about the load. It was put on the boat with its handles resting on the gunwales.

At their destination the boat was reversed into the shore, the cage door facing land. men then left the boat after attaching a rope to the door and boarded another craft that had followed them out.

From the safety of the second boat the rope was yanked to open the door. But there was no drama.

"She stuck her head out, looked around and ambled away into the bush," said Mr. Fraser.

The team now hopes to rescue the remaining five lions on the island and also six zebra, a number of sable and about 50 buffalo—apart from smaller animals like warthogs.

Wednesday 26/9/62

The Rhino Mvara developed a stomach ache, not eating, and no signs of having defecated during the night; put some epsom salts in water but up until 5pm had only drunk a little of it.

May have to drug the animal and give it an enema if there is no signs of any improvement.

7pm gave Mvara a shot of drug, roped his legs and gave him an enema by means of stirrup pump, & 4 gallons luke warm soapy water; put arm up its rectum, and pulled out hard lumps of droppings.

I gave it 2cc of antidote, and by 10pm he was eating again.

An entry from Rupert Fothergill's diaries of 26 September 1962, detailing giving a rhino an enema.

THE OPERATION NOAH TEAM

Operation Noah was led by Rupert Fothergill, who was a senior game ranger in the Rhodesian Department of National Parks and Wildlife.

Dozens of men were involved, most from Parks, including some government department veterinarians, two vets from Uganda experienced in large animal immobilizing techniques, and an extraordinary team of dedicated and brave black and white Africans, many of whose names have sadly been lost to the passing of time.

(Top row) Archi Fraser, Ron Van Heerden, Paul Coetzee
(Bottom row) Graham Child, John Williamson, John Condy

Top: Rupert Fothergill, Tiger Teguru, Tommy Orford, Middle: Frank Junor, California, Len Harvey,
Bottom: Barry Ball, Rex Bean, Tinkey Haslam, Right: James Kwava

Team members came and went over the years – only a handful were there from beginning to end.

Archi Fraser	Barry Ball	**Trackers**
Bruce Austen	Peter Jones	Langton
Rex and Gwen Bean	Greg Gregory	California
Tinkey Haslem	Allan Savoury	Tembo
Peter Moore	Paul Coetsee	Phineas
Graham Hall	Graham Child	James Kwara
Rupert Fothergill	Danie Bredenkamp	Samison
Frank Junor	Mike Van Rooyen	Kadiki
Tommy Orford	Ranger Venables	Tiger Teguru
Len Harvey	Vet. John Condy	
Brian Hughes	Vet. John Williamson	
Ron Van Heerden	Dr. A.M. Harthoon	
Lofty Stokes	Dr. J.A. Lock	
Ian Nyschens	Stewart Claasen	
Boyd Reese	Ranger Turnull-Kemp	

Rupert Fothergill holding a young Duiker

ACKNOWLEDGMENTS

First and foremost thank you to my daughter Kirsten Drysdale for her help with editing and compiling this book.

I would also like to thank John White whom I pestered endlessly to delve into his vast knowledge and memories and also assisted me with contacts related to the story.

Thank you also to Ray Reid (Tinkey Haslam's daughter) and Margaret Haslam (Tinkey's wife), for your memories that you so willingly shared with me.

Thanks to Angela Henderson for her permission to use Ian Henderson's sketch from the book "Fothergill" by Keith Meadows of Crackers for the cover and to Angie Meadows for the same.

Thank you to Tori Stowe for the sketch illustrations used in the Crackers story.

For further information on the story of Operation Noah, the people involved, and to view some of the incredible photographs and film of the events, please consider consulting some of the following references which were invaluable resources during the research of this book.

REFERENCES:

Operation Noah 16mm film episodes – Rupert Fothergill

Operation Noah Diaries – Rupert Fothergill

Fothergill: Bridging a Conservation Era – Keith Meadows

National Parks and Wildlife Management – Mike Bromwich

Kamchacha Rhodesian Game Ranger – Bryan Orford

Personality Magazine 1968 – Bryan O'Donoghue

Kariba: Legacy of a Vision – Jonathan Waters

Kariba: The struggle with the River God – Frank Clements

Animal Dunkirk – Eric Robins and Ronald Legge

Rescue of Rhinoceroses – A. M. Harthorn and J. A. Lock

Thanks to Ang Lourens and friends for planting the seed.

First published in Australia 2025

This edition published 2025

Copyright © Hilary Drysdale 2025

Cover design, typesetting: WorkingType

(www.workingtype.com.au)

The right of Hilary Drysdale to be identified as the Author of the Work has been asserted in accordance with the Copyright, Designs and Patents Act 1988.

All rights reserved. No part of this publication may be reproduced, stored in a retrieval system, or transmitted, in any form or by any means without the prior written permission of the publisher, nor be otherwise circulated in any form of binding or cover other than that in which it is published and without a similar condition being imposed on the subsequent purchaser.

ISBN: 978-1-7640828-7-7

www.ingramcontent.com/pod-product-compliance
Lightning Source LLC
Chambersburg PA
CBHW041647160426

43209CB00019B/1850